Answering the 'Who Am I' Question

Find Your Purpose and Be All You Were Meant To Be

An Ignite and Inspire Series Book

Joy

MJP Publishing LLC

To CJ

You have come so far! I love you, son and am so proud of you!

To Jaycie and Raven

You have both grown into lovely, confident, young ladies! This is so great!

To one of my 7th & 8th grade teachers at Horace O'Byrant Middle School, the late Mr. Norman Alan Davis

You saw a diamond in the coal that I was. You held a mirror up so that I could see not only what should be changed but, more importantly, the good parts of me that I didn't see. Thank you for believing in me and giving me a chance to be more than just a face in the crowd. The seeds that you sowed so many decades ago has paid off. Thank you, sir.

Introduction

Jean plopped onto the couch, dropping her purse and kicking off her shoes along the way. "I hate my life. I *hate* it!" Tears welled in her eyes as she defiantly crossed her arms, looking around the living room with disdain. Taking it all in, she could hear herself breathing, the hum of the refrigerator in the next room as the only other sound. She continued to wonder *Why I am here?? Why do I even get out of bed?*! With that she exhaled loudly, stood up, balled her fists at her sides and grumbled in emotional anguish "ahhhhgrhhah!" She walked, defeated, into the kitchen greeted by the continued sound of the refrigerator and almost as if it understood her, the refrigerator stopped purring as she yelled, "Oh shut up"! Her emotional pendulum swung from anger to defeat and back again as she looked around the kitchen. *Something needs to change* she thought and continued searching the room as though it had answers, and then her eyes caught the passing of a butterfly outside the kitchen window, drawing her attention away from the emotional roller coaster that had just been consuming her. Intrigued, she went outside to see it more closely.

Jean's story is not the exception; it is the rule. Sadly, most people never find satisfaction in life. It seems out of reach, like the ever-flitting butterfly. However, there are times when it will land on your shoulder where you admire it, and then the hopes, dreams, and happy 'what ifs' that you briefly entertain, like the butterfly, are gone. Those represent the happy moments of life; a baby being born, a vacation, a night out with your best friend, a promotion at the job. While those moments are wonderful, they cannot carry us through life. Each day, not just a handful of moments, needs to be a consistent moving toward something, otherwise, you will forever have butterfly on the shoulder moments at best, which isn't much more than existence. No wonder it's so hard to get out of the bed each day or why we procrastinate sleep, hoping tomorrow won't come.

The lifecycle of the butterfly will be our journey comparison and we will also follow Jean as she discovers how to go from hating her life to looking forward to her days. Just as with the butterfly and Jean, the journey for you will not stop there. You will also learn how to continue the cycle of purpose, change, and continued growth and re-creation.

At some point in your life, the laid out for you path of schooling and adults telling you what to do has ended. The problem is that most people get stuck right there. When I say most people, *I mean most.* This doesn't happen just in the teens and twenties when one is "supposed" to be figuring things out. I know many people in their 30's, 40's, 50's and older that have stayed in that stuck place. The thing is, at some point you have grown up – gotten taller, survived puberty, aged to and crossed the imaginary line of child to adult – and now no one tells you what to do next so you wing it and do what you think you should do, or are expected to do, or have always done. This generally does not lead to life fulfillment. So how does one move out of that stage and into something meaningful?

How do you create those butterfly on the

shoulder moments and capture them, keeping them in hand, not releasing them as momentary wonderment? More importantly, how do you have a life full of them? A life of satisfaction, fulfillment, and purpose, which at its core, is who you are. How do you wake up each day in joy not sadness, in thrill not boredom, in excitement not dread, being the person that you were meant to be? That is what you will discover in this book.

What to Expect

- In the following pages, you will encounter specific, step through it now, things to look at, think on, consider, and do. I encourage you to answer the questions or ponder ideas *as you read through the book*. There is no need to rush through each chapter to the Action Steps. Imagine that I am across the table or in the car driving along with you having this discussion.

- At the end of each chapter are questions and action steps. You'll need to answer and do those. Honestly. This is not a magic bullet... *Lemme just read this great book and somehow, I will wake up tomorrow in my happy place.* Instead, think of this book as a workshop. You learn, then do. Repeat.

- You will need something to write on and with. Call it a journal, notebook, stapled pages of loose paper, whatever works for you, but this is necessary, so get those things now.

Things to Keep in Mind

Don't let the simplicity of this be deceiving. In fact, embrace the idea that you can follow these steps and write your own script. Think of it, in about the time it would take you to watch a few movies or binge watch a few seasons of your favorite show, you will be empowered to take the steps toward achieving a life that you want. Yes, it really can happen.

Every book in the Ignite and Inspire series is a condensed version of a single topic based on years of mentoring and generally helping people. These subjects have come up multiple times over the decades and are just as valid now as they were 20 years ago. *It would be realistic to imagine them as a one-on-one session with intense focus* that open doors, windows, eyes, and the world for you to see more, experience more, and love your days more.

Lastly, like all books in this series, it is not an end all. It is meant to wake you up, unfold the road map, and get you started. *Once you are on your way, you will come across resources and people that will help you to grow in that next area or phase of your life.* I'll get you started by providing a resource section for each book on my website[1]. You can also take your journey to another level by sharing your thoughts and questions on the Discussion Page[2] and dialogue with me and others.

This is a journey, and as it has been said, the journey of a thousand miles begins with the first step. So, grab a pen and paper, take a deep breath, and put a smile on your face because the days of hating your life are about to be over. You can do this! Let's get started!

Chapter One

"You cannot predict the future, but you can create it." Peter Drucker

A female butterfly lays her eggs under the leaf of a plant. In one to two weeks, the gestation period is over and a caterpillar eats its way out of the protein rich shell and then the fun really begins! Wildlifetrusts.org defines a caterpillar as "the larval stage of a moth or butterfly. It is the second part of their four-stage life cycle: egg, larva, pupa and adult."

Wait, what?? Did someone just tell me that there is no Santa Clause? *Easter bunny*?! TOOOTH FAAIRY?!?! So, then a butterfly isn't a creature that formed from another creature? It is just, just, a *grown-up caterpillar*? Excuse me for a moment while I unwind that from my mind and sweep up the glitter that just fell from my silly imagination.

Yep, a butterfly is actually just the grown up, nothing magical at all. As you will learn though, that doesn't make the transformation less amazing. The butterfly, in its larval stage as the caterpillar, has a few tiny eyes, stubby legs, very floppy antennae and its sole purpose is to consume. Gardeners would say "destroy" because caterpillars will eat up a plant! The caterpillar looks like a fancy, fat, often hairy, colorful, worm thing and inches along with a purpose that seems to be no more than to eat and shed its outer layers, which it does up to five times. In fact, this approximately three-week portion of its life is just *part* of the journey to becoming its true self. In short, other than the various colors and patterns it wears, how much it grows in such a short amount of time, and the football team amount of food it consumes (ok, maybe a little bit of exaggeration), there isn't anything really fantastic to say about a caterpillar. There doesn't seem to be much more purpose to this creature than to consume/destroy.

Let's look at it in context though. What is the purpose of this short period of its life? To ingest nutrients and grow so that it is prepared for the next stage (pupa), *which has to be successful* if it will reach its ultimate stage as the full-grown butterfly and live out its true purpose, the reason it was born in the first place.

You might be thinking: *Yeah, this is all interesting, but who cares about bugs? Relate this to my dread of leaving the bed every morning.*

Fair request, but first allow me to describe the end result so that you know where we are heading. The full-grown butterfly was once a pinhead sized egg hidden underneath a leaf and then became the boring and seemingly purposeless caterpillar that went through a really hard scenario (metamorphosis) in the pupal stage, and emerged as a contributor, not just a consumer, with abilities like flying and gathering, and even helping humans. In short, once it grew into its purpose, and the tools to navigate that purpose were provided, it was able to live the life it was meant to live. And you can too!

Jean admired the butterfly with its royal blue wings outlined with an even darker blue, and splattered with various shades of beige dots. It sat on a limb slightly above eye level, as though it were inviting her to take in its beauty and participate in its peaceful rhythm, slowly folding and unfolding its wings, showing the amazing designs on either side. She found that her breathing matched that rhythm and her mind wandered. Eventually Jean found herself thinking *How did I get to this place? I have a lot going for me and life is so beautiful; why do I hate it so much?* Then she came out of her peaceful introspection and frustration arose once more. *Why am I here?!* As if cued that the moment was over, the butterfly flew away leaving Jean alone and staring at an empty branch, which mirrored her insides.

Is this where you find yourself? Wondering what it is that you are supposed to spend this life on? Asking 'Who am I' or 'Why am I here'? Needing a reason to take the next step, attend the next meeting, drive to the next destination? You aren't alone.

When you think on your life, it seems like a running story. Because it is. Just as with books, life has chapters and sometimes, it is difficult to realize when one has ended and another has begun, because the story pulls at the same thread and has the same main character. You. We get so engrossed in the 'now' of the story that we don't realize that it is time to turn the page, to journey to the next step.

. . .

What That Looks Like

Many of us know people, or are the person, that never emotionally left the formal schooling season. They still pull pranks, gossip, go day to day doing only the bare minimum to make the grade (or the paycheck) and other things that are considered characteristic of those in the formal school time frame. I know people in their mid 40's who *still* talk about high school, telling the same stories, remembering the same events over again each time they get together and in social media posts. Of course, at that age, the ones that remain close also have other things in common, but it absolutely amazes me how *fresh* high school is in their minds and how those experiences, not always their talents, have directed what they spend their days on. I know a *lot* of twenty-somethings that still see themselves through the eyes of the 16-year-old version of themselves. What do all of these people have in common? They remained a caterpiller, never entering the pupal stage.

Let me ask, do you still see yourself as the jock, geek, lead in school plays, class president, band nerd, homecoming queen, a nobody? Don't give what sounds like the right answer. Answer the truth.

There are too many TV shows, movies, comedy skits, songs, and the like, referencing the distant past as markers of who they are today for it to just be you who is still stuck or at least affected in some way. You aren't alone in this. Until you find where you are, you cannot move to where you want to be, so look inside and answer it. *There is no shame in finding your starting place.* If anything, it is to be commended! It means that you are doing what others won't. Good job!

Side note: Keep in mind that I do not know how old you are, so please set aside any negative that you are tempted to feel and hear the points being made. If you are 16 reading this book, you are *so* ahead of the curve! If you are 96 reading this book, *I am so proud of you!!* And everyone in between, good for you for wanting more! Let's do this!

To recap, our butterfly-in-the-making has come out of and eaten its egg shell and plant leaves around it, and now it is time to move to its third stage in growing up, pupa. This is where the magic of metamorphosis – massive change – happens. It is the next part of its journey which leads to a satisfying and fulfilling life. That is why most people hate their life; because they didn't finish the journey. They are still a caterpillar only consuming and never making it to or through pupal stage let alone to the full-grown butterfly so as to experience life as it was intended, full of contribution, thrill, and wonder. Why? There are many reasons, but the 3 main ones are:

- The distractions of life: a parent died, a baby was born, the job changed, moved to a new city/state/country, personal illness or injury, relationship changes, too many or time consuming extra curricular activities, etc, or maybe you thought you were on the right path, but got distracted by something you are good at and can do well instead of the thing you are great at and love doing. For example, I am very good administratively. Your business would thrive with me in place! However, I lose track of time when I am teaching, serving, and writing, which are the things that I am great at. I am *exhausted* at the end of the 8-hour administrative day and only a little tired after a 12-hour writing, teaching, serving day. I still feel like I have a whole day of work ahead of me (dread) and *zero* sense of thrill or fulfillment at the end of the administrative day, but am satisfied, full, and content after a day doing what I love and am great at.

- In your lifetime you have adopted beliefs and created habits that have not served you well as they limit your perspective of your abilities and most likely, your self-worth. We will touch on this later.

- You don't know how to do it. From the beginning, learning and growing was automatic and at some point, the body was developed and the planned schooling journey was completed. Then you found that the map had ended and you have been driving along without a compass since.

Wherever you find yourself, you are not alone.

There are many caterpillars! The difference is now you know that there is more and are taking steps to get there. Right now, simple is key. Simple gets us started and moving toward our goal. We can always make things better and sharper, but if we wait until we know and understand everything, our life will be that of marking time, a busy 'rocking the chair going nowhere' life. As Kenneth Hagin said, "You cannot steer a parked car", so start where you are right now and keep in mind that part of your success will be learning more and continued growth. We will discuss that later.

Moving Into the Pupal Stage

I recently saw a greeting card with a lovely painted butterfly on it. It read, "There's nothing in a caterpillar that tells you it's going to be a butterfly." The truth is, if the caterpillar judged its future on what it was at that time, it would have laughed and continued munching leaves until it became another's dinner. The same is true for us. If we see only what we have been or are right now, we will laugh at the idea that one day we could fly. *I ask that you keep an open mind as we go through this unfolding of the you all wrapped up inside.* Let yourself get excited even, because you have embarked on an adventure of discovery and becoming! As we continue, any time you feel like scoffing, remember that the caterpillar is not the butterfly yet, and that change, even great change, is normal and natural and *possible*. Let's continue!

Now it's time to set up for the pupal stage. Just like the caterpillar, you are putting yourself into a position and place where the change (metamorphosis) can occur. In order for the caterpillar to do this, it spits out material to attach itself to a branch or sturdy object and then it wriggles out of the last of its exoskeleton showing its hard pupal shell we know as the chrysalis. This is the hard, green thing that we see hanging from a branch or other sturdy surface.

How do humans move into the pupal stage? You establish where you are (connect to the branch), recognize what is inside of you (the chrysalis), and accept and work on what needs to change (metamorphosis).

Action Steps for Chapter 1

In this section, you will do a lot of looking inward and answering questions to see the real you. This is where you need to lean in and take note of what you are experiencing and thinking. Take some time to ponder your answers. Don't just breeze through this section. Roll up your sleeves and get your hands dirty. *This is the workshop portion of the book where real growth begins.* These are the same type of questions and activities I would present to someone sitting across the table from me. Many of them went on to become the butterfly, and you can too!

HINT 1: There are no right or wrong answers.
HINT 2: The more you put in, the more you get out.

First, read through the bullet points below to get an idea of what you will be doing so that you know where to direct your attention and what to note. Then go back and do the work in whatever order feels right to you.

- Sit back and scan your life like you would a horizon. You aren't looking for details, just an overview. Do you see a pattern/s? Do you see a thread/s? Do you see a connector from 'then' until 'now'? Is there a theme? Do you return to the same interests? What regrets are you experiencing? Do/did you have teachers, family, or friends admire how easily XYZ skill comes to you while you think it's just no big deal because "anyone can see a completed dress just by holding up a bolt of fabric"? Are there any defining moments? Did you transition from do as you are told, go to school, do your homework, etc to being your own person, living a life of your chosen path? Or did you just move up a level from your while-in-school job or go to a job that was simply available and you haven't left it?

(Or any other number of before and after scenarios.) Write down what you see and remember, the threads, etc.

- What stood out to you? What moved you? If money, time, and other people's expectations weren't a factor, could you see yourself doing that all of the time or at least having it in your life on a regular basis? What emotions arise when you think of that? Is there a scared-thrill as hope ignites and flickers inside? Do you want to jump up and dance? Slam your fist in the air yelling a resounding "yes"? Are you nervous to let yourself even "go there" mentally... really?... me?... I could be that? As tears of "oh please could this really be real" well up in your eyes? Describe what you are experiencing right now.

- Are you still having trouble getting answers or need to see this a little more clearly? Then let's get *really* real. What if you had only one year left to live, what would you spend your time on? How would you spend your days differently if a million dollars was deposited into your account with the sole instruction of its use as: "Do what you love". Don't start and end with "I would quit my job". Ok, and do what instead?

- What are things that you value or hold dear? What strong character traits do you possess? (Do not assign a positive or negative to these traits as there are two sides to every one of them. As you move through this book, you may find that "you as the aggressive dictator" is just the undeveloped "you as a positive leader" that comes out as you grow and move forward.)

- Look five years into the future of the life that you love. What does it look like? Just write, don't think. Freely get it all on paper. There are no silly answers or wishes or thoughts. Just write, write, write (or type, type, type). You cannot know where to go until you find where you are, and you cannot put together a

puzzle until you have all of the pieces.
Take your time with this.

- Write out what you would like to be said
  of you after you pass from this life. I was
  challenged to do that years ago and it
  jerked the slack out of me. I still have
  that original writing and have built on it,
  referring to it often.

You did it! You found where you are on the map
getting fully into the pupal stage, and are now set up
to experience metamorphosis. *Congratulations!!* This
is where great change occurs by moving you to the
final part of the journey. Head on to Chapter 2 with
me and let's do this!

Chapter Two

"Life motivation comes from the deep
longings of the heart, and the passion to
see them fulfilled urges you onward."
Proverbs 16:26 TPT

Jean turned slowly away from the branch
aware of the emptiness inside of her, longing
for something to fill it. Back in the kitchen,
the refrigerator again humming as it kept her
food cool, she almost envied it. The refrigerator was
doing what it was designed to do. She imagined the
hum being that of profound contentment. Grabbing
a yogurt and spoon, she left the happy – eye roll –
refrigerator and was again in the living room. For no
specific reason, she grabbed her sketch book and
color pencil set before again plopping on the couch.
Her mind wandered to the butterfly and Jean
quickly found herself capturing its likeness on the
empty sheet in front of her. Much time had passed
when she noticed the word drawings she had created

around the butterfly. Coming out of her focused state, she held the sketch pad with both hands turning the page this way and that to read the words she had drawn. *Unattractive, athletic, obsessive, compliant, eager, smart, boring.*

What is this? She wondered and immediately provided her own response. "This is how I see myself!" Jean realized that she had some good qualities, but that she didn't like most of what she saw drawn out before her. Intrigued, she turned the page and started writing what her last week looked like and realized that *most* of her weeks look just like that. She further realized that *she* wasn't specifically boring, that her *life* was boring, that eager and smart are good qualities, and that she only felt unattractive because she didn't particularly like herself, and that set her to wondering why.

Jean set the sketchbook aside and leaned back into the cushions. Long ago forgetting about her yogurt, she went back in time in her mind. She scanned her past like a slide show and saw some of the same stories and themes repeating. The light bulb moment was when she realized that each one of those scenarios presented a choice for her, but most of the time she just went with the flow, never questioning its down the road effects. Jean not only felt regret grip her stomach as she remembered lost opportunities, but she also re-experienced the momentary elation of times when she didn't go with the flow and did things that she truly enjoyed, like art projects and helping children learn to read. She volunteered with the library reading program one summer and absolutely loved it!

As you scanned the horizon of your life and took the Action Steps for Chapter 1, did you have this experience? Maybe you didn't forget about your yogurt, but you remembered how you loved to... how you were good at... the activity that gave you such a sense of fulfillment.

If you have not already, highlight or circle things you wrote down that thrilled you to your core or warmed your face with a smile. What moved you in a good way? What made your heart rate go up? What sent you back in time feeling that rush of adrenaline? What made you want to sing or laugh or clap or dance? What made you... happy?

THAT THING... *that* is part of your purpose. So, does this mean that Jean needs to quit her marketing job and become an artist? No. But what if she takes an art class or attends an artist meet up or simply adds that back into her schedule instead of scrolling through social media for two hours each night? Could she give her art as gifts? People always told her how great her work was. Can she sell it? Can you make money doing what you enjoy? Also, Jean has a creative job. Maybe she can spend some time in a different department more along her skillset and see if a transfer is the needed change. Then she could potentially enjoy, and not dread, going to work. What are we looking at here? *Options.* Now Jean has options, and so do you!

Think of any good book or movie. The character is going about life and *something changes; they go through a struggle,* and then they come out the other side a changed person. Do you see how now, your story is changing, and you get to turn the corner, growing into what you want to be? Ahhh... the power of purpose!!

Jean felt her face and insides grow warm as she remembered specific children that she helped and how much progress they made that summer. She knew instinctively that marketing was what she wanted to do with her days and that sent her mind in multiple directions. Soon ideas were bouncing around her head and she turned to another page in her sketchbook and started making notes of what was coming to her. She could barely keep up with the ideas:

Check with the library about their reading program for children.

Call Mom and see if she still wants to go to the art exhibit next month.

Stop by the art supply store and pick up watercolor paper.

What age group would I like to work with?

Does my job have a volunteer plan where I can use company time to work with non-profits?

Jean wrote faster and faster as ideas and questions and wonderings came to mind. For the first time in, she didn't even know how long, Jean felt alive!

Now it's Your Turn

Take a moment and reflect on these great feelings that have come to you and brainstorm how you can get these activities into your life. Are you like Jean and have a love of helping people learn to read? Write it down. Did the thought of woodworking strike a spark in you? Write it down. Do you wonder what would happen if you finished your law degree? Write it down. I could throw out ideas all day long. Instead, this is your workshop. Set this book down and write ideas and questions and thoughts as they come to you. Don't think about it, just write it down. I call it brain dumping. Just get it on paper and we will sort it out a littler later. There is no time limit. I am not staring at my watch. Jeopardy music isn't playing. This is *your* moment to discover so that you can become. Take the time that you need and savor this moment.

Bonus Information: To clear up any assumptions, the thing/s that you came up with may not be your sole life's purpose, but I can assure you that it is a part of who you are and quite possibly what you are to be known for.

Example: You will still keep your management job and go skiing on the weekends and then win a competition which leads to .... which leads to... which leads to... and now you are a model and love it! You may find the skiing, in this example, wasn't actually your whole or entire purpose, but the *doorway* to your purpose. That is why I keep saying 'part of your purpose'. For now, just start where you are. Get skiing into your life, which will increase your overall life satisfaction with more exciting and happy days than not, and see where it takes you. Life is a journey...

"Joy, is it really this simple?" I have been asked that question (about this and other subjects) *so* many times. And I will grin with a twinkle in my eyes and tell you what I have told all of them: the answer is yes and no.

Regarding this book, finding what thrills your heart, your purpose, that is fairly easy. You are working on that right now. Continue to watch for threads, themes, comments from others, and listen to your inner self when things feel light and wonderful.

Take note of all of that. That is the "yes" part of my answer.

It is possible that you have a list of heart thrillers, tingle makers, and sigh inducers, but maybe you just don't see how you can add that into your life or be that person. That isn't *finding* part of your purpose, that is not *knowing how to implement* it. That and overcoming objections, which all of us will encounter is the "no" part of my answer. So let's fix that.

Where are we Going from Here

We'll touch on some objections, learn what metamorphosis looks like for both the pupa and human, check in with Jean, and then discuss ways to implement your findings. Finally, we will circle back to the egg as we discuss continued growth and personal re-creation, which also answers the "now what" question for anyone, but especially those who feel purposeless after having accomplished what they gave so much time and attention to.

Action Steps for Chapter 2

The workshop continues as we build on what you have already done. You will need your completed steps from Chapter 1 so if you have not done that yet, now is the time. Don't rush through this. You are writing the script of your life *and you are worth the effort.*

- In the section *Now it's Your Turn* we discussed brain dumping. If you didn't do it while reading, do it now.

- Compare what is on the dump list with the things that you highlighted/circled on your previous lists. Is there a theme or pattern? Start putting these things in categories. Jean has two major categories (art and helping children learn to read). I have three. A dear friend has one and another five. It doesn't matter how many you have because every person and every season for every person is different. Just categorize all of your findings without judgement. This is setting the stage, declutters your thoughts, and creates something specific that you can work with.

- Now choose the one category that makes your vary core swell up with happiness (you can do this with all of them, but do them one at a time). Spend some time thinking about how you can put this, or even a part of this into your life as soon as possible. If it doesn't come easily to you, go for a walk without electronics and think, or do that in a bath, or sitting quietly outside. You can also ask someone you trust to help with ideas. Lastly, there is always the internet. You will be *amazed* at how many people share your passion. No kidding. I have a friend who not only plays the accordion quite well, but he collects them too, and he is part of a whole community. Who would have thought?? Please remember that this isn't for you to judge or be negative about. This isn't right or wrong. It is what your heart desires. So what that you never learned to ride a bike? If you want to be a mountain biker, then go learn! Again, you will be amazed at the resources available to you, especially if you just ask for help. Most people respect someone humble enough to ask for help; especially if they too are a lover of that subject. They will usually go out of their way to give you extra help if you are polite and receptive.

- Create deliberate habits. Meaning, don't keep doing what you are used to, but what will move you forward. Set up times to start your forward momentum. Trade out something that *doesn't* help you achieve this new level with something that *does*. Even just a 30 minute internet search for a meet up or group in your area, or a stopping by the bike shop counts. Put in your schedule something toward your goal at minimum several times a week. Remember, this is that thing that makes you want to get out of bed each morning! Sure, you may still have to be a barista by day, but you can be the actress by night at the local playhouse. Step by step, work toward that thrill maker, smile producer, life enhancer. You have no idea where this could lead!

Please share your findings on the Discussion Group. We want to cheer you on and possibly even be a resource for you. Don't go it alone. In the meantime, Chapter 2 is in the bag! Let's keep the momentum and move on to Chapter 3.

Chapter Three

"What the caterpillar calls the end of the
world, the master calls a butterfly."
Richard Bach

Some pages back, I mentioned that there are
habits and beliefs that you have adopted
that have not served you well. The full,
scientific reasons are found in a library of books and
multiplied hours-long lectures. There are a lot of
great resources available to help you dig super deep
into this, and you are welcome to dive into all of that
at some other time, but for now, let's keep going. The
purpose at this moment is to turn on the light so that
you can see what you might be dealing with. As you
go through your days and nights and come across
objections that you cannot readily resolve, I
encourage you to seek out resources to help you overcome them. See my website or ask the Discussion
Group for starting points.

What are some of the big objections or hidden lies we believe that keep us stuck where we are?

Fear of
what people may think
failure (which can also act out as perfectionism)
change
the unknown/not done it before
not being deserving or worthy/not good enough
because XYZ person said so

Become comfortable with your familiar discomfort
There is science to back up that humans generally don't like major change and would even favor staying in an uncomfortable situation so as not to have to rewire their minds to something new, even if the new thing was amazing.

Distracted/Addicted to dopamine
There is an immediate feel good (dopamine) of playing video games, watching TV, scrolling through social media, eating junk food, and so much more. This is extremely distracting, as is getting involved in

other people's drama and other less than ideal ways to spend your time.

Digging these and other limiting beliefs out, making changes to your schedule to add in purposeful activities, adjusting your character to be the person that you want to be, and actually *doing* the new thing or taking the steps to do it, is the metamorphosis part. This is where *huge* change takes place. How huge? Let's look at what happens inside the chrysalis.

Metamorphosis

As explained on biologydictionary.net:

"A great deal of energy and raw materials are required to turn a caterpillar into a butterfly. To make it possible, caterpillars release enzymes that dissolve most of their bodies... the hard shell is required not just to protect the metamorphosing insect from attack; it is required to keep its liquefying body bound together. Not all of the cells are dissolved by these enzymes. Special tissues called imaginal discs survive and they use the soup that used to be the rest of the caterpillar's body for nutrition. By consuming the proteins, vitamins, and minerals – everything you need to build a butterfly – these imaginal discs are able to grow incredibly quickly, developing into the butterfly's mature body parts. The new body has almost nothing in common with the old body. It has new legs, new sensory organs, a new exoskeleton, a new reproductive system. Even its digestive system does not work the same way, since it must now digest nectar instead of leaves. That's all in addition to the beautiful wings."

That sounds fairly complicated and unpleasant (and gross), as the insect is basically liquified and put together anew.

I know that this part can be tough. Just as the caterpillar sheds its layers to accommodate for growth, and the pupal stage is a full breaking down and building new, we must shed the old, let go of the past and what is holding us back and enter into a place where we can become and fully experience who we really are. If you aren't willing to go through liquifying the unnecessary to make way for the necessary, you will not be able to be what you want to be, because you won't have the tools necessary to do what you need to do. For example, the butterfly *must* go through metamorphosis to have wings so that it can fly. Period. There is no way around this.

I would like for you to also keep in mind that the caterpillar shed its skin multiple times before going into the pupal stage. You too cannot expect to be a butterfly overnight, but you *can* expect results. The caterpillar got bigger and bigger over time, then went through stages in metamorphosis until becoming the butterfly. You too have layers and go through times of growth and learning. You won't be a 5 star chef overnight, but you can attend the cooking class once a week and start applying what you are learning as you make meals at home. So keep in mind that this is a step process and that you will get better, learn more, and realize that there is a whole world that you were missing out on.

There was a new energy about Jean as she got ready for work. She realized that she had not turned on the television or scrolled through her phone in the last two days as she researched and allowed her mind to piece together what this new version of her life looked like. She had already made an appointment to see her boss about spending time in other departments of the marketing agency, as well as to see what kind of time off options she had. Her trip to the art supply store had her nearly skipping the isles like a little girl! And Mom was thrilled when she received the art exhibit tickets Jean emailed to her for their weekend together next month.

As she brushed her teeth, that little voice in the back of Jean's head kept poking at her telling her that she might make waves at work if she tries to change too much, and that planning to spend her entire weekend painting was just a waste of time. Jean caught a glimpse of herself in the mirror as she was drying her hands and paused. Thinking back to her horizon glimpse moments, she felt the pang of regret remembering all of the times that opportunities came her way and she went with the flow instead of changing direction. *No more.* Jean turned from the mirror determined that there is nothing wrong with meeting with her boss just to see what her options were and that if she wants to spend her weekend painting, she can do just that!

Again her steps got lighter as she stood up for

herself to her own thoughts. She decided to listen to an audiobook about overcoming those thoughts permanently on her way to and from work. *It's time to take my life back,* she thought decisively. With a smile, she grabbed her purse, and headed off to work.

Action Steps for Chapter 3

It's workshop time! Get out your pen and notebook and let's keep going.

- As you were reading through the objections, did any of them ring true for you? If so, which one/s and what can you do about overcoming it/them?

- Keep at least one, "this thrills me to my core" idea in front of you as you pursue change. Keeping your eye on the prize makes going through any changes worth it. As you continue to do what you love and are good at, it will also make the changing easier and faster. You can look up vision boards and see if that is something you could use to help you along.

- I once heard that decisions are easy when values are clear. Write out your top 3-10 values. This helps guide you toward the person you want to be and keeps you true to yourself when it is decision time. There are a lot of options and distractions out there. These help you to color in the lines and not lose yourself in the process. I have my top five values written in order of importance on a chalk board in different colors by my desk. When I have to decide between two things and cannot quickly choose, I look to my values list to help me decide.

Sometimes growing is an all by yourself thing; just like the chrysalis experience. Most of the time, however, the journey is easier and more exciting when shared with others. Consider joining the Discussion Group and get a conversation started. In the meantime, Chapter 4 is waiting. Let's see life as a butterfly.

Chapter Four

"Nobody can go back and start a new beginning, but anyone can start today and make a new ending." Maria Robinson

Y ou've done the break down phase of metamorphosis by recognizing and starting to overcome objections as you have looked further into things that excite you. Now it's time to build into the butterfly.

Do not wait: the time will never be 'just right'. Start where you stand, and work whatever tools you may have at your command and better tools will be found as you go along.
– Napoleon Hill

> The beginning is always now. – Roy T. Bennett

Hopefully you see the point. It is time to stop thinking, writing, planning, and looking. It is time to start doing things to move you forward. Just like Jean, go on a fact-finding mission. Check websites for classes or activities or meet ups or groups that do that thing. Go to the library or the local coffee place and look at their bulletin boards for events going on. Ask around, share your ideas with friends and family and see if they know of any starting points, or ask on social media.

If it is art related, go to an art store and ask an associate about events, classes, or options they may be aware of. Do you want to learn to ride a horse? Find stables in your area and go there, or give them a call. So what if something doesn't turn out that time? At least you are driving your life in a direction that thrills you instead of just existing day to day. *This is a quest, a journey, a mission! It is ok, and encouraged, to try, test the waters, experiment. This is an adventure!* Peter Daniels (a once illiterate brick layer turned intelligent billionaire) asked in a meeting that I attended many years ago, "What are you trading your life for?" That got my attention. When I heard it put that way, it made me want to make my time and days count.

Pacing

Don't get overwhelmed and feel like you have to go all in at first. It is like a person that starts a weight loss program. They buy a months worth of work out gear, pay for a full year of the gym, throw away all of the food that they know and buy stuff that they are clueless about (how to prepare, what it tastes like, etc) and then the big day comes, they work out, realize how hard it is and then stop off for greasy fast food on the way home. Yes, there are exceptions, but we all know that most of the time that is exactly what happens.

Start small. Just throw on what you own and go to the gym and do a light workout. Eat a meal you are familiar with or a healthier variation that you know that you like. Once you have gone to the gym for a week, buy two outfits or go grocery shopping for a few new things to try. What is better, smoking only half of a pack of cigarettes because you know that you can handle that or continuing to smoke a pack a day until you get up the nerve to quit cold turkey? (Which may never happen.) If you wanna cold turkey it, then go for it! But don't do it because you think that you are lacking if you taper off. Take steps to get to your goal. *Small steps are better than no steps.* **Start today.**

Make the phone call, look up the meeting, drive to the location, buy the book, sit down at the computer, sign up for the class, submit the application, buy the dancing or hiking shoes, go to the audition, set up the appointment... don't wait, just go and adjust as you do. And *if you see it as a quest or an adventure, it is even more fun.*

No Comparing

Do *your* best. Only you know what that is. Don't compare yourself to anyone. And not the you of 20 years ago. The you of two minutes ago. If you fall, get right back up and keep at it. Simple as that. Good job! You've not eaten junk food in three weeks and today had half of one of those fresh baked goodies you smelled as you walked into the house. Good for you for eating just half. And by the way, enjoy the half. You're ingesting it so you might as well savor it.

Celebrate

Congratulate yourself when you do something well, rather it is big or small. Share your victories and keep the momentum going. Don't let that voice in your head talk you out of patting yourself on the back. You went to the gym and walked on the treadmill for seven minutes and even though you feel like you are dying, YOU DID IT! Congratulations! Next time, try the recumbent bike for seven minutes or see if the gym has a trainer that can put you on a "just getting started" program. So what if you aren't lifting a ton or running or slamming out pull ups? *You went and you tried!* No one is a success overnight except maybe those four year old piano prodigies. I am being silly here, but think about it, you stepped out of your comfort zone. That alone is to be celebrated!

This is a Journey

The point is that this is a journey. I am *so glad for you* that you finally have an idea of what you want to do and *so proud of you* for making steps toward it. Do

your best. Enjoy this time. Back to my exercise example, I once read a quote about those that are doing something are lapping those who are sitting on the couch. So, act on your investigative research, take the weekend course, accept the internship, go for it. Don't get stuck in research mode (based in fear). Take the leap! Set the appointment, ask your friend if they want to come along, write the poem, look up the entrance requirements, get the membership, rent the equipment, etc. Get moving and realize that this is from now until... (the rest of your life) *so enjoy the process*. Get after it, yes, but enjoy it. Isn't that the point of all of this in the first place; to get where you love waking up each day? Getting started *is* doing what you love. You don't have to wait until you are the expert to enjoy it.

In short, now is the time to implement what you have discovered. What did you find as options? Did you write it down? Did you sign up for the class or event? Did you attend the meeting? Did you have the dinner, draw the drawing, price the gear, buy the tickets, make the speech, start the blog? Did you open the door? Take the step?

Thinking back to our movie/book analogy, if the main character walked right past the opportunity for change, there would not *be* a book or movie. It would end right there. And so it is with you. Please. Do not stay in the chrysalis. Be the butterfly.

Your Value

I want to add some clarification and a warning. Make sure that you aren't expecting that reaching your goal defines you or is what makes you valuable. *Who you become as you are doing what you love is what should bring the most value and satisfaction to your life.* There is a whole other side of this live your purpose, be who you are meant to be, follow your dreams, subject that I hope can be summed up in this true story (name changed).

John was a very large man who was kind and funny, but miserable inside. Sadly, he was still miserable even years after losing nearly 200 pounds because he thought it was the weight that made him miserable. It wasn't until he started liking himself for who he was and doing things that made him happy (building websites and volunteering in fundraisers), instead of 'I have to look a certain way', that he started to have real joy in his life.

So, if you are looking for the accolades and money and finished product to give you peace in your heart and make you like yourself, you are missing the point of this book. If you need direction or suggestions, reach out to the Discussion Group so that we can help you make adjustments and cheer you on.

Jean was surprise how rude the librarian was when she asked about volunteering for the children's reading program and she was equally surprised that they had a wait list for people to volunteer. Feeling bummed she opened the refrigerator and realized that she was humming along with it while looking inside for dinner ingredients. She pulled out leftover lasagna and salad mix, and giggled under her breath as she used her foot to close the door. Oh how life had changed, and she didn't even have any answers yet! The meeting with her boss went ok, but she realized that even if looking at other departments didn't turn into anything, her new perspective was helping her to enjoy what she had in front of her day-to-day at the job. Something about just pursuing her passions kept her mood light and even more importantly, hopeful.

Dreamily, Jean put the fork full of salad up to her smiling lips, thinking about tomorrow when she gets to attend her first painting class. That bite of salad tasted extra good!

Action Steps for Chapter 4

Are you ready to start wriggling out of the chrysalis and see your beautiful new wings? Are you excited about the new abilities that you are about to have? Great! Make the following happen, today if at all possible.

- Chapter 4 was riddled with starters. What is your starter? Now do that. Get it on the calendar or if possible, do it right now.

- Can you set up a step 2 as well?

- What can you do to ensure success? Do you have a friend or have you found a group of like minded individuals that will step it out with you? Or at least stand on the sidelines rooting for you? Have you put things on the calendar, bought the yoga mat, etc? Do whatever you need to do to ensure success. *Make it easy to take the next step*.

- This part is fun, but hard at first because we aren't used to it. *Savor the moment*. You wanted to try indoor rock climbing and there you are, all hooked up to the safety equipment and staring at the odd shaped handle things (fake rocks). Instead of being scared, turn that into being excited. Rest one hand on the first "rock" and let a thrill go into your hand and up your arm. The physical experience for fear and excitement are the same. Just tell yourself which one it is that you are supposed to be feeling and your brain will do the rest. Did you just make your first gourmet meal and it doesn't look so pretty. Who cares? Take a picture of that first effort and then enjoy each bite. *Enjoy this time. You get to do*

what you love!! And like I have said both
in this book and to countless people face-
to-face: you'll just have to believe me on
this, you have no idea where this could
lead! Exciting!!!

- Consider writing down Peter Daniel's
  question "What are you trading your life
  for?" and putting it somewhere that
  would normally be a distraction to you,
  such as a sticky note on the TV remote
  or game controller.

Are you ready to wrap this up? Then let's go to
Chapter 5 and make it happen!

Chapter Five

You've done it! You have gone from a caterpillar, just consuming and not being or doing much of anything (or at least anything in your eyes and heart), to a butterfly. You have your wings and now the possibilities are endless!

But Wait, There's More

The butterfly is fully equipped to do what it was intended from the time it was an egg attached to the underside of a plant. And you too can continue to recreate yourself, finding new adventures, refining areas of your character, learning new things, sharpening your skills, and being a contributor and setting a positive change in the world, even if it is just your world (home, office, town, etc). This is *your* story. Write it (or draw it or paint it or sing it or build it... just make it happen).

The thing to remember is just because you did it once doesn't mean you are done. You can "lay the eggs" of your life, re-create yourself and your life, over and over and over again! Keep the cycle going by continuing to learn and grow. Continue removing any negative residue and focus on building your strengths. Continue experimenting and stepping out. Keep going through doors and see where things lead. Don't get complacent. Even once you are fully in your purpose, there are still ways to expand yourself and contribute.

Where to go From Here

From here we will touch on ways to continue growing, being a contributor, and how to handle the "what's next" question, including post goal sadness.

You will most likely be in awe of the world around you that you have missed all of this time as a caterpillar. Rather you went back to college, started a new job, picked up a hobby that you love, started volunteering, whatever it is, you will meet new people and encounter experiences *that enrich your life in ways that you would never would have imagined* during the days of scrolling through social media hour after hour.

Besides learning your craft (rowing, teaching, reading faster, whatever you have chosen to pursue) better, you will also become a better version of yourself. You will find your self esteem has grown, you will value your time and your word more, you will find that shallow things no longer fulfill you, and you will want to come up higher and grow in depth as a person of character.

You can continue your path of growth and re-creation with books (written and audio), podcasts, classes, and activities that change your mindset and the way that you see yourself and your life. Where can you go for these? This list can get you started:

- Your library has physical books and most likely has digital (ebooks, audiobooks) resources as well.

- Ask people in the groups that you have become a part of for resources and suggestions.

- Depending on what you are looking to do, a community recreation center or community college could have answers.

- Groupon is a resource for inexpensive ways to dabble in something before you go all in (archery class, wine tour, riding lessons, etc).

Whatever you choose to use, I encourage you to use balanced, highly suggested resources until you are more familiar with the subject to know what to look for. This can also help you not get overwhelmed. Remember, this is supposed to be fun. If it is a drudgery, then you are either not on the right path or maybe that particular resource isn't for you. Keep it simple. Enjoy your journey.

Contributing

We admire the butterfly not just for its amazing transformation (and finishing what it started), but also for its contributions to the world. They, along with bees, help to pollinate so that we can have flowers and food. They let scientists know if there is an environmental problem they should look into because butterflies are sensitive to habitat, which means that they are also an indicator of a healthy environment. Some butterflies eat aphids helping the gardener and some eat waste. Because they are pretty and interesting, they contribute to bio tourism. We use their life cycle in life lessons and encouragement. And scientists have learned about antibiotics from butterflies and used them as a model for technological breakthroughs.

The question is, now that you are not sitting in the recliner hour after hour doing mindless, meaningless things, what *are* you doing as your part to make the world a better place? Here is a sampling of ideas to get you started:

- Volunteer doing something along the lines of what satisfies your soul and puts a smile on your face. Choose something that you look forward to doing. If you do it out of obligation, you are missing the point.

- Every day (or throughout your week) send a text or mail a card to someone and let them know that you are thinking of them. It doesn't have to be extravagant or fancy. The effort is what most people will remember. This also has the added bonus of enhancing relationships.

- Hold the door open for someone, smile at people, let a waiting car go ahead of you in line, pay for someone's meal, listen for the response to your "how are you" question of the cashier or waitress. Be nice.

- Do you remember how someone took you under their wing when you first showed up to the new event/activity/class? You might still be a newbie, but you could at least be available to the next new person who joins that group and maybe even learn more as you go, and possibly make a new friend.

I think that you get the idea. So let's move on to

two things that you may encounter as you proceed: post event sadness and the "what's next" question.

Post Event Sadness

While post event sadness can happen after an exciting, life changing event such as summer camp or a weekend motivational retreat, it is usually experienced after completing huge milestones that you wrapped your life around for years, like finishing graduate school or selling a business that you built up over many years. When that sole purpose for most of your waking hours is no longer there, there is a letdown type of feeling. The real high and then real low. What is going on? The high or rush you felt when the finish line was crossed happened because your body was flooded with feel-good hormones like endorphins and serotonin and now, they are gone. Also, the pleasure-seeking neurotransmitter dopamine is activated when we actively pursue goals and now that the race is completed, no more dopamine (related to that activity). So, what do you do?

- You can talk with someone about how you are feeling by reaching out to a friend, colleague, counselor, or anyone that you are comfortable sharing this with. If your emotions have dropped severely, you should definitely take this step.

- One way to reduce the effect of post event sadness is to not apply any of your self-worth to achieving or not achieving the goal (see previous chapters). *You are not your end goal.*

- You can move on to what is next, which recharges you by getting you back into the game of something exciting to wake up for each day. Having a steady cue of things that you want to accomplish or levels you want to attain, keeps you on a path that has high-five happiness along the way, and usually keeps you off of the up and down roller coaster. Having a cue of goals makes finishing something more like a marker tapped as you pass on to the next item instead of a full stop which leads to the letdown. For example, if you train for a marathon as part of your

ultimate goal of winning an Iron Man
competition, winning the marathon is
more like - yahooo! CHECK! And
ooooon to the next level of training, as
opposed to "well now what do I spend
my evenings on"?

What, "What Next" Looks Like

Sometimes the goal is years, or decades in the making
so it may not occur to you to have a plan B. So let's
fast forward to you have done something long term
that is now over, or reached that goal and are
wondering what's next, *now what?* You retired, the
children are raised, the screenplay has been written
and sold, you won the gold medal, sang for the
queen, traveled the world, patented and sold your
invention, opened the gallery, etc.

The first thing to remember is that just because
you've met the goal, life isn't over. Some have called
this the success trap. That previous version of you
has achieved their goal and you don't know what to
do next. The answer is so simple it might make you a
little dizzy.

You set a new goal. *However*, you need to adjust

your perspective or at least remind yourself of some things.

The 'I've met my first goal' version of you (who you are right now) is the one that needs to set the new goal because the 'goal accomplished you' is not the same person as the 'pre-goal accomplished you'. When you set that first goal, you were a whole different version of yourself and your desires and excitements may have changed since you started that now accomplished goal. You have learned new things along the way and have grown into a different person than you were pre-goal. You are now the Olympian, Mom, Graduate, Business Owner, Chef, etc. Now it is time to make a story for and live the life of the 'goal has been accomplished you', the you of right now. What does that person want to tackle? The framework of that previous goal, or your life as you knew it, doesn't exist anymore because it is no longer consumed with that goal. You crossed that finish line. So what race are you training for now? What picture will you paint now?

Your new story starts up where the old one left off, like a part 2 or 3 of a series. You have the start of your new story because you are living it right now, and now you define how you want this next story to end. That doesn't have to mean the end of your life, just the end of that cycle, that goal frame of view. Chart out your new path. How? Use what you have learned in this book. What thrills your heart in this season of your life?

So go ahead, scan the horizon, look for threads and patterns. Look around your today. What tingles your senses today?

Action Steps for Chapter 5

You are almost done! Are you excited, you brilliant butterfly?!

- Have you found a resource/s that will help you hone your craft and move more toward the person that you want to see in the mirror?

- What way/s could you contribute to beautifying your world?

- If you still need help, have you asked for it?

- If possible, consider outlining a cue for yourself. You aren't obligated to it, but having other ideas at the ready will ensure that you are always forward moving and reduce your chances of getting stuck in a rut or post event sadness.

Once you have finished these actions steps, turn the page and let's find out what Jean did with her research and initial steps.

Epilogue

Jean was beaming as she got into her car. Volunteering at the elementary school once a week was easier to get involved in than she had imagined although there were a few hoops to jump through like a background check, and getting permission to take off work an hour early on Thursdays. It turns out that her company does have a program that allows her to volunteer without compromising pay. She applied and was approved! Her little student Mary is such a joy to teach and is making great progress overcoming her reading difficulties.

As she drove home, Jean's mind was running other possibilities like volunteering on the weekend teaching adults how to read. *I have a degree. I wonder what would be necessary for me to teach an adult reading class at the community center?* Her mind kept coming up with ideas.

Now home, Jean entered the living room and smiled as she set down her purse. Her heart swelled as she saw her art hanging on the walls, one in the works on an easel, and those done and leaning against the bookcase one in front of the other. Picking up a water color piece, she knew that her aunt was going to love it for her birthday! Piece by piece she looked at them, admiring her work, loving her life, and as she looked up, the computer in the corner of the room caught her eye. Seeing the abundant artwork, more than she could ever display or give away, Jean wondered if selling her art was an option. Putting the painting down, she walked to her computer. *I wonder what will happen if...*

And so it can happen for you! But not if you do not start. Dear reader, you have unfolded the map, located at least part of your purpose, and thought of ideas on how to get this into your life. You have begun to overcome objections, taken action steps, and let the hope in your heart burn brighter. You have come this far. The metamorphosis has taken place. It is time to wriggle out of the chrysalis. No go, be, do. Fly butterfly. Fly!

Thank you for letting me be a part of your journey! I would be ***over the top*** if you sent your life cycle adventure to me!!! Remember, we celebrate every victory, no matter the perceived size! If you would like to connect, please visit www.MsJoys Place.com or better yet, let all of us rejoice with you on the Discussion Group at www.facebook.com/ groups/msjoysplace.

Notes

Introduction

1. www.MsJoysPlace.com
2. www.facebook.com/groups/msjoysplace

Bibliography

BD Editors. (2019, October 4). *Metamorphosis.* Biology Dictionary. https://biologydictionary.net/metamorphosis/

Identify caterpillars | The Wildlife Trusts. (n.d.). https://www.wildlifetrusts.org/wildlife/how-identify/identify-caterpillars

Jomard, A. (2019, November 22). *What Happens Inside the Chrysalis of a Butterfly?* Sciencing. https://sciencing.com/happens-inside-chrysalis-butterfly-8148799.html

Living, G. (2022, February 21). *Why butterflies are beneficial to the environment.* Good Living. https://www.environment.sa.gov.au/goodliving/posts/2018/12/benefits-of-butterflies